*The Mass in Other Words*

# The Mass
## In Other Words
A Presentation for Beginners

by Dom Hubert van Zeller

This edition is based on the 1965 printing
by Templegate Publishers.

This edition republished 2025 by Silverstream Priory
with the kind permission of Downside Abbey.

New material and graphic design copyright
© 2025 by Silverstream Priory.

All reservable rights reserved for the new material
of this edition. No part of the new material of this
edition may be reproduced or transmitted, in any
form or by any means, without permission.

*Nihil Obstat:* Ralph Russell, O.S.B., *Censor Deputatus*
November 27, 1962
*Imprimatur:* Christopher Butler, *Abb. Praes.*
November 30, 1962

The Cenacle Press at Silverstream Priory
Silverstream Priory
Stamullen, County Meath, K32 T189, Ireland
www.cenaclepress.com

ppb 978-1-915544-43-8
ebook 978-1-915544-44-5

Book design by Nora Malone

Cover design: Silverstream Priory

*For Pepita,*
*who asked for it*

# *Contents*

1. The Main Idea . . . . . . . . . . . . . . . . . . . . . . . . . . . 1
2. Ways of Going About It . . . . . . . . . . . . . . . . . . . 11
3. Why the Mass Is What It Is . . . . . . . . . . . . . . . . 19
4. How the Mass Has Been Built Up . . . . . . . . . . . . 27
5. Effects of the Mass . . . . . . . . . . . . . . . . . . . . . . . 33
6. Changes in the Mass . . . . . . . . . . . . . . . . . . . . . 45
7. The Place of Holy Communion . . . . . . . . . . . . . . 53
8. 'It's Easier for You Priests'. . . . . . . . . . . . . . . . . . 59
9. The Mass and Christian Unity . . . . . . . . . . . . . . 67
10. The Mass and the Rest of the Liturgy . . . . . . . . . . 73
11. Summing Up . . . . . . . . . . . . . . . . . . . . . . . . . . 79

# 1

# *The Main Idea*

You have probably read in some holy book or other that the Mass is the centre of the Catholic's day. It is true that there can be no more important half-hour in the forty-eight half hours which make up a complete calendar date. But you can go further than this and say that the time of Mass is the most important in the century, in history, in life. It is Calvary all over again, and nothing more important could happen in this world than the redemption of man by the crucifixion.

When you go to Mass you do not go to spend a holy half hour in church; you go to take part in our Lord's act of prayer and praise to the Father—in his act of redeeming mankind from sin. Your attendance at Mass is one of your main duties as a Catholic. But you should go not only because it is a duty, but much more because it is an opportunity—it gives you the chance of joining very closely in what our Lord is doing on the altar. (And that is exactly why the Church has made Mass-going at least once a week a Catholic duty.)

So the main idea is not to hear something holy being said, not to see something holy being performed in vestments, or even to be present while something holy is being done by a fellow human being who happens to be a priest. The main idea is to be one with the act and the mind of our Lord in giving his perfect sacrifice to the Father. Nothing could be more holy than our Lord's intention, and when you join your own intention to his at Mass you are doing something infinitely more pleasing to God than anything holy which you could think of doing on your own.

A lot of Catholics go to Mass on Sundays either because it would be a serious offence against God not to, or because it would look odd to other people if they stayed away, or because they have become so used to going every week that it has become mechanical. Such reasons for Mass-going are not good enough. Such reasons are good enough as far as they go—because even to go automatically to Mass every Sunday shows at least that a good habit has been kept up—but they do not go very far. If a person's fidelity to Sunday Mass rests on nothing more solid he will find excuses eventually for not going as regularly as he used to. Fidelity to the Mass must rest on a firmer foundation. There must be an understanding of what is going on and a love of our Lord Who is the central figure.

So avoid the idea that you come to Mass simply to follow the words out of a book, trying frantically to catch up with what the priest is saying, and to be able at the end to pat yourself on the back for having been obedient to the Church and having "heard Mass". "Now *that's* over" you would tell yourself with relief, "and now I can get on with my ordinary day and forget about Mass until I have to go again." Not at all a good idea to have about the Mass.

Nor is watching the actions of the priest the main thing—because you could watch a televised showing of it and not say a single prayer or take any part in it whatever—while still less is listening to the music or a sermon the main thing. The main thing is trying to get so near to our Lord in spirit that you do what he does, and pray what he prays, and love as he loves. This is really the whole point about your going to Mass, and if you understand this much you will quite easily pick up whatever else you are expected to know and do about it.

In other words, your best way of assisting at Mass ('assisting' gets nearer to the idea than 'hearing', because although it sounds stiff and old-fashioned it does at least show what you are supposed to do—you are supposed to help) is to hand yourself over, with our Lord, for the service of the Father. The Mass is in the most real sense a "service", and not simply a ceremony. It *serves* the Father. And because the Mass is offered by our Lord, it serves the Father perfectly. Other services, whether held in church like Benediction or given privately to God like acts of self-denial, are not guaranteed perfect as the Mass is guaranteed perfect. Where the act is our Lord's own act, and the prayer is our Lord's own prayer, there is no room for the slightest imperfection. It is bound to be infinitely good in the Father's sight.

So you see what is wanted of you when you come to Mass. You are asked to assist by sharing your whole self with our Lord, by being ready to help in any way He may want, by joining in as far as you can with what He is doing on the altar. And what is He doing? He is doing exactly what He did when He offered Himself for crucifixion and gave up His life on the first Good Friday. The Mass may not look a bit like what happened at Calvary, and since our Lord is now in heaven with His Father He cannot suffer when His sacrifice is repeated on the altar, but the Mass and Calvary are nevertheless one and the same thing. Not painful any longer, as rendered by the priest and ourselves, but absolutely paying for the debt of sin and absolutely glorifying to the Father.

At this point you may feel like saying: "But much as I would love to offer myself for crucifixion in some distant future when perhaps I shall be holy enough to make such an offering sound true, I cannot honestly pretend that I am ready yet. Does this mean that, because I am not giving myself as our Lord gave Himself to the Passion, I am not really with Him in the sacrifice of the Mass?" No, however holy you were you could not take on our Lord's Passion just as He suffered it. All you are asked to do is to offer yourself for whatever *your* passion may turn out to be, and to unite your intention with His in the suffering of it.

By taking up our cross we take up His; by taking up His cross we take up ours. The more we understand this, the more we understand the Mass; the more we understand the Mass, the more we understand this. The Mass and the cross, our Lord and us. And because our Lord on the cross and in the Mass is atoning for the sins of all the world, we too, having a share in His cross and in His Mass, bring something towards the same work. It is not only our own sanctification that we help along when we go to Mass, but the sanctification of others too. This fact should be very comforting to us, because it means that everyone's Mass-attendance helps everyone else. It means that on the days when we are not assisting as well as we might, our losses are being made good by the people who are attending their Masses (perhaps on the other side of the world) with extra special generosity.

So the great thing, then, is to put your intention into our Lord's, your soul and mind and body into what He is doing at the Mass. In this way every Mass becomes a communion between you and God, even if you are not receiving Him sacramentally, and a communion also between you and the other members of His mystical body. We are all one in Him, and nothing teaches us more about this truth than going often to Mass and receiving Him often in Holy Communion.

Even as you read this page you are probably saying to yourself: "Yes, I know all that. It is a wonderful thing to know that our Lord catches up my prayers into His, and that the Mass is an infinite store of merit and love which I can dip into and offer to the Father. But the trouble is I forget about these things when Mass is going on. The words of the missal don't excite me much, my fellow-worshippers in the church look so ordinary and not a bit what I would expect members of Christ's body to look like; the altar is far away and I feel quite out of touch, the priest doesn't go about the movements of the Mass as our Lord must have taught the apostles to go about them, and there I am at the end of Mass without having made a proper prayer to God from start to finish."

A lot of people feel just that, and these are real difficulties. But however much you feel that the time of Mass has been time wasted, you have at least been there, meaning to join your offering and your will with our Lord's, from the beginning to the end. You have not wanted to think of other things, you have not given up and talked to the person next to you or read a magazine, you have not walked out and had a look at the pamphlets in the porch. So long as you have not deliberately let the idea of being with our Lord in His act of sacrifice fade from your mind, you have not wasted your time. You have been a partner in His work, even if you have not been attentive to the partnership all along.

Partnership with Christ sacrificing, fellowship with Christ in praising the Father, pouring out with Christ the infinite merits of the Passion over all the world. That is what your presence at Mass has meant. You were not just being *present*, as you might be present at the giving out of prizes at school, but in intention at least, you were being *active*. It is as if you were distributing the prizes yourself, on the platform with our Lord, and as if the prizes were all of infinite value because consisting of our Lord Himself.

You cannot expect to remember all this while the Mass is going on, but God does not ask you to have a good memory. He asks you to have a good will, a right intention. Your will and intention are bound to be good and right if they are in line with His. So the important thing is to set your mind in the right direction towards God at the start of Mass, and to try to keep it there. If following the words out of a missal helps you to keep your mind fixed towards God, follow the words of the missal. There is no better way of doing what our Lord does than using the words which the Church uses when He does it. But do not feel that repeating word-for-word the part which is read out by the priest is the only way of assisting properly at Mass. (In another chapter we shall be going into the various ways in which we can pray suitably at Mass.)

If you cannot be expected to remember a lot of holy truths while you are attending Mass, neither are you expected to understand all that there is to know about the Mass. One of the Mass's names is "the mystery of faith", so you will never know *everything* about it. The whole point of calling something a mystery is that, though it may be grasped, it cannot be made absolutely clear. The whole point of faith is that it believes without doubting a truth which still is more or less hidden. As *the* special mystery of our faith, the Mass will always be beyond our perfect understanding.

Besides, how much did the apostles perfectly understand what was being done in front of them by our Lord at the Last Supper? There is nothing to show that they were given an instruction on the Blessed Sacrament beforehand. They were told simply that the bread which our Lord broke was no longer bread, but the actual body of Christ, that the wine in the cup was changed into His blood. Understanding this, the apostles understood quite enough to make them active partners in our Lord's act. They were sharing in what was, with the crucifixion which was to follow, the first Mass. Their share in the Mass did not depend upon their knowledge of its theology, but rather their knowledge depended upon their readiness to share our Lord's intention in what He was doing.

In the same way it can be asked how much of the crucifixion which took place later was fully understood by those who were present at it. No books had been written about it, no sermons had gone into the theological meanings and details. Even now, when the Church's greatest minds have explained all that can be explained about Christ's redemptive death on the cross, how much do we really know about this mystery of God's love? When we have said that the Second Person of the Blessed Trinity died for man on Calvary we have said just about all. The fact that He *was* the Second Person of the Blessed Trinity puts Him and His infinitely perfect act beyond our human understanding.

So do not feel that your lack of knowledge need be an obstacle either to your getting the best out of the Mass or to your putting the best you have got into it. The more ready you are to go along with our Lord, the more you will come to understand. But it will be in that order: readiness leading to knowledge. Then, when you understand more, you will find yourself becoming more and more ready to go along with our Lord all the way. The one will help the other, and you will be mounting to God by two ladders at once—with one foot on each.

If studying the theory of sacrifice helps you to love the Mass, go ahead and study. Anything that draws you closer to the Mass should be followed up. For those Catholics who find that a study of its history and its inner meanings makes the Mass seem dry and distant, it is better to get hold of a few hard facts (like the ones we have been talking about) and pray about them. The main thing to be avoided is a feeling of stiffness towards the Mass—as if it were a subject on which you had to pass an exam. Once you start lecturing to yourself about the Mass you begin to lose sight of it as a prayer. Above all the Mass must be alive to you.

# The Main Idea

It is grace that brings the Mass alive, but there has to be a certain amount of help from you. It is for you to find out the best way of helping grace in this matter of making the Mass a reality in your life—in making it the chief reality in your life. A soul who shapes his prayer, his life, his whole being— and this includes his work, his trials, and his love of other people— round the Mass is set for heaven. The Mass fits out such a soul to appear before the throne of the Father. It would be true to say that for a Catholic to become holy without the Mass would be as impossible as for a Catholic who loved the Mass not to become holy. (Think that one out, and perhaps it will help you to value the Mass more.)

## 2

# *Ways of Going About It*

We have seen already that the way which the Church puts before us in the matter of assisting at Mass is the way of the missal. So we cannot go wrong in making the missal our main support. We should learn to find our way about it, to make sure that we know where to turn to next, to take trouble over the bits which at first do not seem to make sense. The missal is not an easy book to make friends with, but, unless it becomes our favorite prayer-book, we shall have very little to fall back on when our own prayers run out. In the missal there is enough prayer-material—and by "prayer-material" is meant the stuff of our prayers—to last us all our lives.

Also we must remember that most of what is printed in the missal is the inspired word of God. This cannot be said of the ordinary prayer-books that are written to help out our devotions and religious practices. A lot of the missal's pages are filled with pieces out of the gospels and epistles, a lot with quotations from the psalms and the writings of the prophets, a lot with prayers especially composed for the Mass and used by the faithful since the early centuries of the Church. So we would be foolish if, just because the language of the missal seemed old-fashioned and stuffy, we put away the missal before seriously trying to get to know it. The language may take getting used to (and certainly is more dignified and stately than what you are reading at this minute, and more suitable to the solemn character of the Mass) but the prayers themselves can never be out of date. People have to be patient with the missal. They get flustered by it at first, and want to pick up something else instead (a rosary, for instance, or an illustrated pamphlet about some especially exciting martyr) but, if they persevere with it, they will find that it grows on them, and that they will always want to take it with them to Mass.

Having said all that, we must be careful not to go to an extreme with our fidelity to the missal and make a superstition of it. The missal is not magic. It is not a sort of prayer-wheel which does the praying for us. Nor is it a guide-book which takes us through the lands of the liturgy. Nor is it a glorified catalog to provide us with devotions to the saints. Nor is it a holy calendar which warns us of the coming feasts and the Church's seasons. It is not even a collection of prayers more or less surrounding Holy Communion. The missal gets its name from being a *Mass-book*, and, just as the Mass is not a service which prepares a soul for Holy Communion and arranges for suitable prayers to be said after Holy Communion, so the book of the Mass is more concerned with the sacrifice of the Holy Eucharist than with our receiving the sacrament of the Holy Eucharist. This does not prevent our using the missal while preparing for Holy Communion and making our thanksgiving after it. On the contrary the prayers of the missal, especially those from the Canon of the Mass, are found by most people to be the best of all Communion prayers. It is just that we shall be disappointed if we expect the missal to be a book of piety and devotion.

In fact there is nothing flowery or hymn-booky about the missal. It goes straight to the point, and faces you with the big eternal facts of religion. It calls you to penance and puts before you again and again the thought of God's mercy. (If you went through the missal counting the number of times "mercy" is mentioned you would find it came oftener than any other word.) It has a lot to say about punishment and death, but has a lot more to say about love and eternal life. It goes on a good deal about temptation and sin, but always there is the idea of grace which is stronger than temptation and sin. The missal does not let you off by any means, but still it is the most encouraging of books because right through all the hard parts runs the blessed note of hope.

But following the Mass with the missal is, for all its advantages, a matter of reading with the eye and (if it happens to be a dialogue Mass) repeating with the lips. Sometimes you may feel that you can follow Mass better without the use of words at all, either read or spoken. The words are only there so as to spark off something in the mind. By themselves the words are no more than printed signs and uttered sounds. Prayer does not *have* to be sparked off by words. Remember that the definition of prayer as it stands in the catechism is "the raising up of the mind and heart to God": nothing about the printed signs and uttered sounds. It is not the syllables and sentences that make the prayer, but the direction of the mind and heart.

This means that on occasions (not always but sometimes) it is a good idea to give the missal a rest and try to go direct to our Lord in the Mass with nothing but your thoughts. Desire is the chief thing to aim at: desire for God Himself, desire to be one with Christ's purpose in the Mass, desire to help all mankind with your Mass-attendance, desire to respond generously to the graces which are all the time pouring off the altar into your soul. Yes, that would be as good a way as any of assisting at Mass: just lining up the best of your thoughts and desires with those of our Lord. And perhaps not saying anything.

Another good way of assisting at Mass is the middle way between a word-for-word use of the missal and this following by head and heart which we have just been looking at. If it bothers you to take up a half-and-half practice, drop it after trying it a few times. But give it a trial because for many souls it is felt to be the answer to their difficulty. Since most of us are half-and-half people anyway, the chances are that a method which is partly speaking to God in words and partly pondering about the things of God without words will be helpful to almost anybody.

You go about it like this. You follow the Mass in the ordinary way with the missal until you come to a sentence or an idea which gives you something to think about, and there you stop. While the Mass goes on, you hang back with your special thought for as long as you feel drawn to pray about it. Sometimes an extract from the Mass can keep you praying in a Mass-minded way from the beginning to the end. You may not have been following each part of the Mass as it came along, but you have dipped into the treasuries of the Mass and taken out enough to keep you paying your debt of praise to God.

Say, for instance, you have followed with the missal as far as the *Gloria*. You remember that this was the song of the angels at our Lord's birth, and you take a closer look at it. Then you work your way slowly through it, pausing and thinking at each full stop. You notice how the phrases are short and clear—designed, it might be said, especially for this kind of *pondering* prayer. 'We praise Thee...we bless Thee...we glorify Thee...have mercy on us...receive our prayer...Thou alone art holy...Thou alone art Lord...Thou alone art almighty...Jesus Christ.'

You could do the same with the *Pater Noster*, with the *Agnus Dei*, with the *Domine non sum dignus*. This way of praying through the wording of the Mass needs a bit of self-control because it depends on not rushing. It also means you have to keep your eyes open to discover passages which will be interesting enough to dwell on. Such passages may be from any part of the Mass—an extract from the gospel of the day or the verse of the offertory—and you will find that you can get into the way of collecting favorite passages. It will be a great help in prayer to have such passages ready so that, when everything else fails, you can fall back upon them.

It will make a significant difference to your Mass if, every time you hear *Kyrie eleison* or *Dominus vobiscum*, you can connect it with something you have thought about and made your own. The English in your missal has shown you what the words mean, but the grace of God in your mind and heart have shown you a lot more that they can be made to mean. What the English does is only to translate; what you and grace together do is to apply. The translation is nothing like as important as the meaning, and very often you can get at new meanings by applying the translation in lots of different ways—to yourself, to particular friends, to special intentions.

The thing to aim at in this way of slowly going through the Mass is to make the text mean something special to *you*. The Church's prayer, by your meditating on it, becomes your own. It becomes part of you. That is what the Mass is meant to do: it is meant to enter into you as you are meant to enter into it. You *belong* in the Mass, and the Mass *belongs* in you. How can you feel at home in the Mass if its prayers are cold distant statements and not close personal realities?

When the priest turns round before the Preface and says *Orate, fratres,* he really means 'Pray, all of you brethren'. Nine times in the Mass he says "The Lord be with you", and this is not just a salutation like 'good morning'. You do not have to race on with the next prayer at once: you can linger on the words and make as much of them as you can. If you spent the whole of Mass saying no more to God than "Lord, I am not worthy to enter under your roof, but say only the word and my soul shall be healed" you would not have wasted your Mass-time. There is evidently enough in the words '*Sanctus, sanctus, sanctus*…holy, holy, holy' to keep the angels and saints in heaven fully occupied in prayer—and infinitely happy at the same time—for ever.

## Ways of Going About It

So if ever you feel that being at Mass is always the same, and that you would please God much more if your prayers were different every time, and that repeating things over and over is just a waste of time because you cannot pay attention properly…well, if these are your thoughts, you can remind yourself that the blessed in heaven do not do too badly with their over-and-over prayer and that this must be the way of praying which God likes best.

3

# *Why the Mass Is What It Is*

You have probably used a magnifying-glass to burn holes in a piece of paper or a leaf or someone's hat. In such an operation there are three separate forces at work: the sun, the magnifying-glass, and you. The heat and the light come from the sun; the lens of the magnifying-glass brings the sun's rays into focus; you hold the glass in such a way that the point of light does the burning. Now in the Mass there are also three forces at work: God, the wording and action of the Mass, and you.

Just as the sun is the most important part in burning holes with magnifying-glasses, so God is obviously the most important power in what happens at Mass. Next after the sun comes the lens. Without the lens you could not bring the light and heat, which is spread out all over the place, to focus. So without the liturgy of the Mass (which means more than just the ceremony and the music) you cannot bring the life, teaching, prayer and death of our Lord into one single act of sacrifice. Lastly, there is you. You have to play your part in the Mass as though you were holding the handle of the magnifying-glass.

If you do not hold the handle properly, if you get bored and hold it at any old angle, if you let your body or your shadow get between the lens and the sun, if you smear mud all over the magnifying-glass, you will never get that pin-pointing of light and heat which does the work you want. The *power* is there: God and the grace of the Mass. But you have to be there too. And you have to be helping—"assisting"—at what is going on.

The Mass, then, brings to bear the infinite love of God. God reaches mankind in any number of ways, but, just as a lens draws together the spread-out rays of the sun, so the Mass catches up into itself God's countless blessings to man and lets us have them in a concentrated form. It also of course catches up into itself the countless prayers which are offered by the members of Christ's mystical body and hands them on to God. The magnifying-glass can work in both directions. Through the Mass comes grace to man, and through it again comes man's response to God.

The idea of sacrifice having a two-way effect is to be found in the Old Testament as well as in the rites of other ancient religions. The animals which were slain in the Temple, for instance, were offered to God by man in worship and in atonement for sin. This was one side of the sacrifice. The other side, God's side, was shown when the priest of the week came from the altar and sprinkled the faithful with the blood of the sacrificed victim. Blood was understood as life. So the sacrifice meant two things: man giving life to God, and God giving back life to man. The tremendous difference between the Old and the New Testament sacrifices is that with us it is the life of our Lord and not of a calf or a lamb that is offered to God, and that it is the body and blood of our Lord which we receive from the priest at the altar. The Mass is what it is because it completes and perfects the idea of religious sacrifice. There is nothing more perfect that can go up to God from this earth than the sacrifice of Christ. There is nothing more perfect that can come down to us from heaven than what the sacrifice of Christ has merited for us.

If you have read as far as this in the book, and have not just landed by accident on the page in front of you, you will see by now why it is that the Church insists on having us assist at Mass at least on Sundays and special feasts. The reason is not that a fixed space of time for saying prayers is guaranteed once in the week and on other occasions when attendance is thought by the Church to be necessary—if this were the case any other religious service would have done just as well—but that anyway at certain regular intervals Christ's prayer is ours and ours is His. The Church wants to be quite sure that we get right into the act of Christ offering Himself on the cross for man, and the Church knows that neither by Benediction, by the rosary, by the stations of the cross, by the recitation of the psalms or by meditation on the Passion can this be fully brought about. The Mass does bring it about—and hence our Sunday obligation.

If it were simply a matter of feeling compassion for Christ in his sufferings, we could satisfy our obligation by staying at home and trying to stir up in our hearts a deep spiritual pity. Reading about the crucifixion, looking at pictures which show our Lord on the cross between two thieves, hearing sermons about the events of the first Holy Week, seeing the happenings of the gospel story acted on the stage: all these things could give us something to go on in the matter of sympathising with Jesus, the Man of Sorrows. But God wants something more out of us than sympathy. And if we attend Mass properly, He gets something more out of us than sympathy. He gets our wills, which mean more to Him than our feelings. He gets our obedience, which means more to Him than the warmth of our devotion.

"Christ was made obedient unto death" says St. Paul, "even to the death on the cross." By being obedient to the Church's law (whether about going to Mass or about anything else) we are taking on something of Christ's obedience. If our Lord stooped so low in His obedience as to "take the form of a servant"—God becoming the servant of man—the least we should do is to offer willing obedience to the Church, becoming humble servants of God. The least we can do is to try to match (as best we can, even if it is from a great distance away) our Lord's surrender to the Father's will.

We too should try to live out our lives with Him on the altar, ready to be handled by human beings in any way they choose. Just as our Lord gave Himself over to the Jews and the Romans, just as He gives Himself over in the Blessed Sacrament to people who, if they wanted to do so, could easily misuse the sacred host, so we should offer ourselves in the Mass for whatever treatment we may receive from human beings.

What else but this do we mean when we talk about "sharing" Christ's life, and "reflecting" the cross, and "participating" in

## Why the Mass Is What It Is

Christ's work? These words must *mean* something, must mean more than merely sitting back and enjoying the benefits which come to us through Christ's merits. All the books that are written about the Mass tell us that we are to place ourselves in spirit with the host on the paten and with the wine in the chalice, and if this advice is to make any sense at all we are expected to be in readiness with the readiness of our Lord for whatever comes.

The prayer which the priest says while mixing the water with the wine just before the offering of the chalice has this to say: "Grant that by this mystery we may be partakers of His divinity Who was willing to be made a partaker of our humanity." No ordinary prayerbook would have dared to claim anything so extraordinary. It is amazing enough that our Lord should be willing to "partake of our humanity", but it is still more amazing that by this mystery of the wine and water which is about to be performed on the altar *we are to be made partakers of His divinity*. And because it is the missal which tells us this, we know the whole weight of the Church's authority stands behind it.

So the Mass is what it is not simply on account of its being highest on the list of Catholic services as performed by the Church's priests. It is highest on the list of Catholic services because it is the only one which is performed by Christ Himself. Some of the things which we do in obedience to the Church are good because we are told to do them (like not eating meat on Fridays); others we are told to do (like going to Mass) because they are good. If we were not commanded to go to Mass on certain days we might stay away and so miss the greatest possible graces which our souls can receive.

One thing we can do by way of making the best use of the chances that are given us in the Mass is to offer, together with our Lord and with ourselves, the needs of the whole world. And in among the needs of everyone alive and dead (because the souls in purgatory can be helped by our Mass-prayers better than by any other prayers we may say for them) we can put the intentions of those whom we love especially and those who have asked us to pray for them.

Remembering always that the Mass is not like a machine which gets us what we want if we press the right switch, we should at the same time be able to trust more in the Mass's power to meet our needs than any other. In the Mass we have not only our Lord's own intercession working for us, but the intercession of our Lady and the saints as well. It is comforting to know that here in the Mass, which perfectly expresses what we are taught about the communion of saints, we link up with the prayers of souls in heaven, on earth, and in purgatory.

In case, after what has been said in this chapter, you should feel confused at the very richness of the Mass's treasures, in case you should feel that there was almost too much to think about and pray about, you can bring the whole thing down to one very simple act of faith and love. At the back of your mind (to be drawn out and looked at when you are feeling stale) you can keep what the catechism tells you about the four ends for which the Mass is offered—namely, praise, thanksgiving, atonement, petition—while in the front of your mind you can pray something like this: "Lord, take my Mass-prayers and shape them as You will…I believe all that is taught me about the Mass…

but I shall only be distracted if I *think* about all that is taught me about the Mass…teach me simply through the Mass to love You and serve You…I ask for nothing else but love…and I know that this, more than anything else, is what You want to give me."

4

# *How the Mass Has Been Built Up*

This chapter is going to be more of an instruction on the Mass than a help towards fixing your attention while Mass is going on. So if you are pretty sure you will not be interested in learning how the Mass came to be what it is today (and for a lot of people the subject would be a boring one) you can skip this part of the book and go straight on to the next chapter. The next chapter is certainly more important—though even in this one there may be some things which make you understand the Mass better and so make it easier to keep your mind on what is going on at the altar.

The first priests, the apostles, had very little to go upon when Mass was celebrated in the early days of the Church. They knew they had to unite themselves in mind with our Lord, priest and sufferer of the Passion, and that they had to repeat certain important words and actions which they remembered from the Last

Supper. They knew that when they "broke bread" (at that time the Mass was called "the breaking of bread") with the intention of fulfilling our Lord's command "do this in commemoration of me" they had in front of them the Body and Blood of Christ, and that the sacrifice was the same as that which had been offered on Calvary. Whatever instruction on the subject they may have received from our Lord between the Resurrection and the Ascension—and it is only a guess that He taught them any more than what they knew already—the apostles, with memories of the Last Supper and Calvary still fresh in their heads, had quite enough to begin with.

Soon, with congregations of the faithful forming round the Mass, it was decided that an informal celebration might lead to all sorts of problems and that in any case a fixed ceremony would be more worthy of such a sacred mystery. If each priest could choose his own prayers with which to surround the offering and consecration, where would be the unity which was to be one of the marks of the true Church?

So quite early on in Christian history the rulers of the Church looked about for a suitable and dignified pattern of prayer into which the Christian sacrifice could be put. Now since the apostles had been familiar with the Jewish arrangement of services, the obvious thing was to take over from Hebrew tradition the frame they were looking for and make it fit the Christian way of worship. The ceremonies of the Old Law were remodeled to serve the New Law, and the converts from the older religion who now turned to Christ were spared a whole lot of puzzling performances which might have put them off.

## How the Mass Has Been Built Up

As it was, the converts were able to feel just as much at home in a church as they had felt in a synagogue. What made them feel still more at home was knowing that our Lord was really there present among them in a way in which the Father had never been present in the old days.

Anyway, you can see how the Mass came to follow the order which it follows today. There were differences, of course, between Hebrew worship and ours— apart even from the main difference, which was the victim itself—but the idea of spacing out the prayers, psalms, readings from the scriptures, blessings of offerings and so on goes back to the first centuries of Christian history. We sometimes think how much nicer it would be if the Mass had remained exactly as it had been celebrated by the apostles after our Lord's death. How much easier it would be to keep attentive if we were just sitting round a table—praying with the priest and watching him as he bent over the bread and wine to say the words of consecration. How much closer this kind of assistance at Mass would bring us to the Last Supper. Yes, that is true, but on the other hand we have been able to give to God more obedience and faith by attending in the way that the Church has arranged for us to attend. What we have perhaps missed in the way of feeling near to our Lord at the supper-table and following, close-up, the action of sacrifice, we make good by submitting to the rules laid down by Catholic tradition.

Whenever something which a few people do together spreads to something which a lot of people do together, there has to be a more careful order about how they go about it. A game which about six people play has to be planned more exactly when it is played by twenty or thirty. Four or five friends meeting for a meal can help themselves, but a dinner party of forty or fifty would be a complete mess if the guests helped themselves and sat where they liked and did not keep to the order of the courses. In the same way the Mass has become organised. The bread became a host, the cup became a chalice, the table became an altar, the supper-room became a sanctuary.

You will often hear the objection that, with the Mass as it is performed in full display today St. Peter would not, if he walked into one of our Cathedrals on a big feast, be able to see any likeness to the Last Supper. That may be true, but the point is not whether St. Peter would recognize the same sacrifice under all the ceremony, but whether you and I do. If we do, then we are all right. We are not asked what we would think if we were St. Peter; we are asked what we are thinking as you and me.

So it is a matter of getting to the heart of the idea and not getting stuck in the outward trimmings. Ceremony and music and vestments are meant to draw us *to* the real meaning of the sacrifice, not to draw us away from it. But we can, if we are foolish, let these things come between our souls and true prayer. True prayer is always to be kept as the main object. We go to Mass to pray with our Lord and not to think about the things which help us to pray with our Lord. You may be sure that, if St. Peter or any of the apostles were close enough to the priest to hear the words of consecration, there would not be any mistake about what was expected. Nobody who had been at the Last Supper would either mistake what was going on or would get so tied up in the outward trimmings as not to pray with our Lord.

In the days when the Church was still what would now be called an "underground" movement the Mass was divided into two parts: the Mass of the catechumens, and the Mass of the faithful. The catechumens were the people who wanted to join the Church but who were not yet ready to be received. Since they were taking instructions and had not learned about the main mystery of the Christian religion—which often had to be kept secret because of anti-Christian spies—these catechumens were allowed to be present only for the first part; until after the reading of the gospel. The gospel could be considered as part of their instruction, but from then onwards only the baptised Christians could be present. The doors were shut, and the second part of the Mass—the important part which was made up by the public profession of faith, the offertory, the consecration, the communion—went on.

Until about the middle of the third century the Mass was said in Greek—the *Kyrie eleison* is the part which is left of this—and then the official language of the Western Church was changed to Latin. In the days of the Greek (or "Byzantine") Mass, the people who were to be prayed for by the faithful present at the sacrifice were mentioned out loud by name. The names were read out from two boards which folded on a hinge and were lined with wax. These boards were called "diptychs".

But even when the Mass was changed from Greek to Latin, there were still a lot of things that had not been finally decided about its celebration. For instance it was left to the priests to decide how often in the day to say Mass. We are told that Pope Leo III (who ruled, if dates interest you, from 795 until 816) said Mass as often as nine times a day.

The rules which have been laid down as to how, where, and when the Mass has to be said have not changed much over the past few hundred years. It looks as though changes may come before long, and, if they do, we shall have the consolation of knowing that they are brought about by the Holy Spirit and not by the fads and impulses of human beings. The really important parts of the Mass cannot be changed, and we shall always know that in joining in the holy sacrifice of Calvary we are doing the most worthwhile thing we can possibly do on earth.

5

# *Effects of the Mass*

If you see someone beating a gong you may notice that for a little while after the last stroke the noise goes on. If you put your ear close to the flat of the metal you will hear it ringing faintly quite a long while after the ordinary gong-noise has stopped. These after-noises are called vibrations, and we are told by scientists that vibrations of sound, even though our ears cannot pick them up beyond a certain point, go on and on and on.

The Mass is like that. The actual celebration of a Mass comes to an end at a particular point; the priest goes into the sacristy; a server comes in and puts the candles out; the congregation goes home to breakfast. But the effects of that Mass, the vibrations, go on and on and on forever.

So it would be a mistake if we were to get up at the end of Mass and say "Well, that's finished for today." The act of the Mass may be ended, but the effects should be carried over into the rest of the day. Now what are these effects of the Mass? There are many, but because we could not go into them all without having a much bigger book than this one to do it with, we can take the two main ones and try to improve ourselves on those.

Clearly if our Lord's act in the Mass is that of self-sacrifice, it is this act which we should carry away from the Mass every time we go to it. Self-sacrifice should, from going often to Mass, become a state of mind. Having offered ourselves with Christ in the morning at the altar, we get into the habit of offering ourselves throughout the day at the various happenings which come along. This does not mean that we are all the time saying "Here am I for whatever suffering God wants me to endure." Such a state of mind might make us think more of misery than of love. No, it means that we are ready for God's will in whatever way it may show itself to us during the day, whether it comes as a pain or a pleasure or as something very ordinary between the two.

But the effects of the Mass do not come on their own, automatically, without any effort on our part. The effects have to be looked for, and got hold of, and worked up into a deliberately accepted way of going about things. Say you are out in the rain and get wet. When you come into the house your clothes are still wet. The effects of the rain are there, whether you like it or not. The effects of the Mass are not like this at all. If you can imagine something so silly, it would be like coming in from the rain and being dry the moment you opened the door of your home: you would have to get under a shower if you wanted to go on feeling wet. In some sort of way like this you have to make a deliberate effort to keep the effects going when the downpour of the Mass's graces has come to an end with the last *Deo gratias*.

## Effects of the Mass

So you can see that of all the effects of the Mass the effect of self-sacrifice is perhaps the hardest to keep up. But because it is at the very heart of the Mass and at the very heart of our Lord's teaching, it is something which we are given special graces to learn and practice. Earlier on in this book there was a bit about our Lord's obedience, and how we should offer ourselves together with Christ in the Mass for the perfect fulfillment of the Father's plan. Obedience and self-sacrifice are one thing—or rather two sides of the same thing. The submission which we learn from the Mass is not grudging obedience which perhaps we feel inclined to give to school rules. It is the submission which we see Christ giving to His Father's will. This was not in the least grudging; quite the contrary. Our Lord's submission was infinitely generous and willing: it was self-sacrifice. Once we have got that, namely, the idea of giving in completely, and out of love, to the Father's authority, we shall no longer find ourselves giving a grudging obedience to anything or anybody.

So becoming more and more Mass-minded, we become more and more ready to see God's will in whatever comes along, more and more ready to obey, more and more trusting in the power of grace. The Mass is felt to cover everything that happens, and *as* things happen we are reminded of the offering which we made of ourselves earlier on in the day during our Mass. Read over the prayer which the priest says as he holds up the paten with the unconsecrated host on it. Read over the prayer which he says when he raises the chalice with the unconsecrated wine in it. Then read over the prayer which he says immediately afterwards, bowing down before the host and the chalice. He prays in a spirit of humility, obedience, and charity that the offerings in front of him may be received by God as an acceptable sacrifice this day for himself and for the whole world. Submission, sacrifice, charity. You could hardly have anything more Christian than that.

You do not have to guess for long before you know what the other most important effect of the Mass is likely to be. Yes, it is charity. Although everything about the Mass should remind us of this, just as everything about the life of our Lord should remind us of it, there is often a complete misunderstanding of how the love of God which we give in the Mass is linked up with the love of others which should flow from the Mass.

In the first place you must have noticed how the prayers are made by everyone together and not by each of us apart. It is *Dominus vobiscum*, "the Lord is with *you*" and not "the Lord is with *thee*." It is "*Orate, fratres*"; "Pray, *brethren*" and not "pray, *brother*". We go to God in a crowd, not just alone. This does not mean that He thinks of us as a crowd—not a bird falls to the ground that the Father is not concerned about, and of how much more interest to God is a human being than a bird?—but that He wants us to worship Him as members of Christ's body. The whole body, head and members, worship as one.

That *Dominus vobiscum*, which, as we have seen, is said nine times during every Mass, is not put in for something to say. It really means something. It is as though the priest were trying to keep the congregation awake at intervals by making them realise that God *is* with them and that they must do their best to be with Him. It is as though he were saying at the same time to God what our Lord said at the Last Supper to the Father: "I pray that they may be one, Father, as you are in Me and I as in You."

So if you think of the Mass as a private devotion of your own, at which a lot of other people happen to be present who are busy with *their* private devotions, you are thinking of it in the wrong way. Just as the priest puts a drop of water in the wine before offering the chalice, so our thin and watery prayers mingle with the whole prayer of all the faithful, whether in the church at that moment or not, and mingle with their strength. Just as the priest sweeps the tiny particles of the Host into the chalice, so we, tiny particles of Christ's body, are swept into the common pool of His precious blood to be presented to the Father in an infinitely valuable sacrifice.

If you look carefully at some of the things which are used in the Mass you will see how this idea of giving worship to God all *together* and in *charity* with one another is put to us again and again. The candles are made from wax, which is the work of countless bees bringing each its own small effort—and notice that the lighted candle burns low, as it were sacrificing itself in giving light to what is going on at the altar. The oil which has anointed the altar is the work of many olives which have lost their own shape and colour in producing the particular fluid which is wanted for the consecration. The grains of incense melt into one another in sending up before the throne of God the kind of holy smoke which tradition has made part of religious service. The bread itself, soon to become the body of our Lord, is made from many separate ears of wheat. The wine itself, soon to become the blood of our Lord, is made from many separate grapes on the cluster. In everything about the Mass, and not only in the words, we are being told that we must keep together in charity; in charity and in Christ we sacrifice ourselves for the good of the mystical body as a whole.

The Church likes to teach by signs as well as by spoken and written instructions, so we should be looking out for hidden meanings in what seem to be quite ordinary acts. Often we miss a message because we do not keep our eyes open. Often in the design on a vestment, in an unexpected pattern carved on the front of an altar, in an arrangement of lines and colors which look as though they had been put there just anyhow in a stained glass window, lies a whole sermon. God likes us to search for His truths, so He hands them to us rather wrapped up. But they are always wrapped in more or less transparent paper so that we can understand what they reveal. So it is important to look out for the signs and not to take them simply for granted. If you do not understand what they are meant to represent, ask someone to explain. You have often seen the emblem of a fish. Have you ever asked yourself what it stands for? (It was painted and carved on the walls of the catacombs as a special secret sign for the followers of Christ because the spelling of the Greek word for 'fish' gave the initial letters of the phrase "Jesus Christ Son [of] God Saviour".) Have you noticed the pelican which is shown piercing its breast so as to give its blood to its young? (Not difficult to see why this is a Christian sign.) There is the triangle which stands for the Holy Trinity. There is the heart which of course stands for love. There is the anchor which stands for hope (an anchor thrown up into the heavens, so that we can feel securely moored to eternal life), and there are the letters AΩ which means that Christ is "the first and the last, the beginning and the end" of all things.

A list could be made of the many ways in which the Mass makes religion more real to us, but when you really come to the heart of the Mass you see that it means living in Christ and Christ living in us. The altar becomes the platform of our charity—love constantly passing over it from Him to us and from us back to Him again. It is the meeting-place between our souls and God: from it He speaks to us and feeds us, from it we offer our prayers and our needs to Him, so important did the altar come to be in Christian worship that it was thought of as an image of Christ Himself.

In the Old Law the altar was mostly connected with death and destruction. In the New Law the altar came to be more than just a table on which a slaying took place: it was the threshold of new life. Christ is truly sacrificed on our Christian altars, but it is a sacrifice which brings a new revelation of Himself. The Mass does not reject Christ's life; it renews Christ's life.

After all that has been said so far in this book, you will see how the Mass and Holy Communion are bound up with one another. Though in receiving our Lord outside the ceremony of Mass we receive Him "whole and entire", we should try to combine our Communions with our Masses. It is at Mass more than at any other time that we both communicate and are communicated to, that we both impart and receive the spiritual waves of one another's charity. As one of the faithful you are not so much being treated to a helping from the same dish as others, or being handed slices from the same loaf; you are receiving the one Christ and *all* that is Christ.

It used to be a practice at one time for popes to send out fragments of the Host from their own private Masses to bishops and priests in the neighborhood. The idea was that the sacred particles, containing the one Christ and the whole Christ, must bring unity and fullness to the Church. The bread of Christ is leavened in common charity, all the crumbs of Christ's priests being brought together in one holy communion. This papal distribution of the Blessed Sacrament used to be called the *fermentum*, which means "leaven".

At this point you may be struck with the thought that the priests of the Church come off so much better than the faithful. Always the first care seems to be for the priesthood. Why cannot the faithful share more in the privileges and graces of the Mass as they seem to have done in the early Church? The nearest a boy can get to the sacrifice is to serve Mass, and a girl cannot even do that. Why is an ordained priest so far above all other ordinary people? We know that the priesthood is a special order and that the priest is set aside for a particular service of God, but could not the faithful be given a more real part to play in the sacrifice of the Mass?

If this is the kind of thing you are thinking, you will be glad to read what Pope Pius XI, speaking to a pilgrimage group of boys and girls who had been present at his Mass, said about their common prayer at his altar. He spoke of "that sacrifice which you, together with us, have offered *as indeed you have* to God."

These words tell us how close the faithful's offering can be to that of the priest—to that of Christ's Vicar Himself.

So when we read in the gospel that our Lord told His disciples to "do this in commemoration of me", we can console ourselves with the knowledge that though only the ordained priest can bring about the change from bread and wine to body and blood, the ordinary man, woman, boy or girl need not feel excluded: in some way, though the Church has never defined exactly in *what* way, the faithful partake of the priesthood.

So when our Lord said "do this in commemoration of me", he meant, *firstly*, that the consecration was to be repeated by priests until the end of the world, and, *secondly*, that lay people were to enter into the action. Notice that our Lord did not tell His disciples to "say this in commemoration" of what He was doing, nor did He tell them to *think* it or even to *preach* it. He told them to *do* it.

In the same way lay people as well as priests are told to do what Christ, in the person of the priest and victim, is doing. They are invited to "re-present" His sacrifice. It is as if our Lord were saying to us all "As I am present here in the offering of the Mass, I want you to be present too. I am wholly present, leaving nothing out. My divine and human nature are at work in this redeeming sacrifice, and I expect My followers to be wholly present also. Not half present, following with their eyes only or with their ears only or with their lips only, but present with their hearts and souls."

When you are watching a game you can tell which players have their hearts in what they are doing and which are there because their names happen to have been on a list. You can tell the ones that are wholly present on the field from those who are merely going through the movements of playing. In our own attendance at Mass we can tell which days we are there with our whole hearts, and which days we are just loafing through. It is not enough to go through the movements. The entire person, I, must act alongside of the entire Person, Christ.

You can see, again, why the Church insists so much on weekly Mass. It is not because Mass is a suitable sort of Sunday duty, but because Mass is meant to be part of life. Mass is not just a detail which prints one day in the calendar in red while the other days are printed in black. The calendar may be saying "that is a day when you have to go to Mass", but the Church is saying "the prayer of Christ is going up to heaven every day and on that particular day you have the chance of gaining the extra merit of obedience by going to it. So, to make certain that you do go, we put the duty upon you and it is a serious sin if you stay away."

To be a good Catholic you have to do two things at once: you have to look back and learn from the beginnings of Christianity, and you have to look forward to see what opportunities and dangers lie ahead. Very often it is by looking back that you learn how to meet the present and the future. So in this matter of the Mass—and particularly in this matter of daily Christian behaviour flowing out from the Mass—there is the account in the second chapter of the *Acts of the Apostles* of how "all they that believed were together, and had all things common…continuing daily with one accord in the temple, and breaking bread from house to house, they took their food with gladness and simplicity of heart, praising God and having favor with all the people."

If you take that little account of early Christian life to bits, and think about the sentences as they follow one another, you get a scene which is as vivid as a film sequence. The faithful were determined to cling *together*; they did not hoard whatever belonged to them but were eager to *share*; they allowed no day to go by without *prayer*; they made the Mass the centre of their lives and the meeting-place of the whole community; and lastly they were a contented lot, winning others to themselves by their simplicity and prayerfulness and love. You could not have a better picture of what Mass and Holy Communion can bring about in a group of people.

The force of the Mass makes just a difference between a crowd and a congregation, between a mob of people and a flock of souls. From this you can see that it is not the building of the church or chapel that makes the congregation—any more than it is the fence round the sheep that makes the fold—but the shared worship of the souls who come there to be with our Lord. Whether Mass is offered in a barn or in a basilica, it is the prayer of the universal Church and in spirit it includes many millions of worshippers. Perhaps we make too much fuss of the four walls which enclose the altar, and forget that the altar is more important than anything which surrounds it. Perhaps we make too much fuss of the parish and its boundaries, and forget that the parish exists for the souls who are included on its lists. Everything about the Church should get us back to the main idea of Christ giving Himself to souls and souls giving themselves to

Him. If the word "Church" brings to our minds the thought of rules to be obeyed, doctrines to be learned, bishops and priests to be reverenced, devotions to be practised, *and does not bring to our minds still more the thought of Christ* then we have only a one-sided understanding of what the Church is all about.

Now you can see why the Mass is made so much of by the Church, and how it teaches us all that we need to know. You can see why our love of the Mass must lead to fidelity to the Church, and how we receive from the Mass the strength to live out our lives as serious and prayerful Catholics. A great French bishop and preacher said this about the Mass, and it is something which we might remember when we feel ourselves getting slack in either our attendance or our attention: "The most important fact in the history of the world is Jesus Christ, and the most important act in the history of Jesus Christ is the continuation of the Crucifixion in the Mass."

6

# *Changes in the Mass*

We have seen in the chapter before this one how the Mass is a corporate act on the part of all the faithful together, joining with our Lord in His sacrifice to the Father. Now if it is an expression of what is called social and spiritual unity, it is also an expression of social and spiritual growth. Growth and change are a part of life itself. Human bodies are always adapting themselves, getting older, sometimes showing new signs and sometimes shedding old ones. The person inside the body remains the same person throughout the changing process of life, but in outward appearance he may change so much that people who knew him at one time may find him hard to recognise at another. In the same way organisms and societies develop and take new shape. Civilization has to progress or it is doomed.

Many of our Lord's illustrations give this idea of a growing, altering, purifying, perfecting, and intensely alive Church.

Remember the references He made to the leaven, the seed, the vine. These are expanding things, things which look different at the end from what they looked at first. Even the parables of the wineskins and the talents speak of altering conditions. New environments call for new approaches, and if we are to live in a moving world we cannot sit still ourselves. 'These are my times,' said the Roman poet Martial, 'I must see my times.' Not only must we see our times, we must see how we can fit into them so that God may be glorified. They are His times too, as well as ours, and He has decreed that we should belong to them—to these particular times and to no other.

So when in our own time we learn that the Mass is to undergo changes, whether of language or ceremonial or both, it is not for us to say "Why can't it be left as it was?" Perhaps it has been left too long as it was, perhaps it would have meant more to the faithful if it had challenged them to a more progressive understanding of its meaning, perhaps now we shall be more on our toes to see it properly in the context of our everyday twentieth century lives.

What is it that we dislike about the idea of these liturgical reforms? Is it not having to sacrifice our own convenience? We have cherished a particular form of worship which has become more ours than it had a right to be. We have become too comfortable in it. In spite of all that we know about the Mass, it is easy to look at it from our own point of view instead of from God's. The Mass was not invented for the purpose of creating an atmosphere in which Catholics might find familiar prayers coming easily. The Mass is God's inspired worship of Himself.

It comes from Him and goes to Him. It is a moving, living, all-embracing sacrifice. It would accordingly be foolish to say "I don't want to move, thank you, because I find I can pray quite well as things are."

The way to correct most of the mistakes which we are liable to make in life is to mount above the personal level and try to see things as they are in the sight of God. In this question of liturgical changes it ought not to be too difficult to see God's hand directing the new regulations. If God wants to have His sacrifice expressed differently, He must be allowed freedom of choice. It is after all His sacrifice. We must not think that we know best. There is divine purpose behind every decree, not human officiousness. We must not think of a school of experts dictating to us. The experts are the Holy Spirit's secretaries and office boys. We must listen to the experts and respect them—they have been selected by the Holy Spirit for the work—but we must know that they are not getting all their information out of books. The direction to their studies is being given by God, and the destination which they are pointing out to us is divinely appointed. Their decrees are not infallible but commanding our obedience.

The principle behind the whole liturgical movement is not simply to update an old-fashioned usage but to bring worship into life and life into worship. In the past thirty or forty years the doctrine of the mystical body of Christ has been put before the faithful and has become familiar to them. What this doctrine amounts to is that as members of Christ we draw closer to one another in charity, and at the same time, by reflecting the head of the mystical body, fulfill our own personalities. Living in Christ we lead lives of enormous opportunity: everything that we do can be raised to a supernatural level. Just as our Lord's incarnation supernaturalised the natural, so all that is natural in our lives can be transformed, because of His incarnation and our part in His life, so that it becomes infinitely worthwhile. The liturgy helps us to see this and act upon it. The liturgical movement comes just at the right time. In a practical way, and through the forms of worship, it brings the doctrines of the mystical body to bear upon the complexities, great and small, of ordinary existence.

The liturgy is designed to be realistic and is not just a fad or fashion. It brings the faithful closer to the essential mysteries of religion, closer than the faithful have been for centuries. So close that they can speak the inspired words of worship in their own language, and learn to participate more intimately in the movement of the Mass. Nor is this a one-way movement, an expression of man's worship to God. The liturgy is meant to stress the mutual or two-way communion: the relationship is active at each extreme. God pours out grace: man pours out response. If we do not learn this from the Mass we miss its implication.

Where human relationships are concerned the correspondence is through signs and symbols. Mostly through speech and writing, but also by means of gestures. We shake hands, wave, pat people on the back, punch them in the nose. These outward manifestations declare our minds; they reveal *us*. They represent an exchange in which, for better or worse, we give ourselves away. Where our relationship with God is concerned the correspondence is again largely conducted by means of signs and symbols. In the Mass we have God giving Himself away in sacrifice. Christ uses signs and symbols by which to express His love for man and the atonement which He offers to the Father. The outward forms of the Mass declare Christ's mind; they reveal Him. But it does not stop there. They are also designed to reveal us. There is an exchange. The Mass invites us to give ourselves away. It asks for the real me, and the more closely I offer myself with Christ in sacrifice the more real a person I become.

So whatever regulations are yet to come with regard to ceremonies and the use of the vernacular, it is as well to remember that they are planned with a view to practical, intimate, and personal participation. The signs and words do not guarantee that we express ourselves at our highest possible level, but they give us every help to do so. Our Lord for His part expresses Himself fully in the Mass; there is no holding back here; He does not deal out Calvary with reservations. It is just our side of the relationship that we need worry about. We need to see that the exchange really is an exchange—in His terms.

It seems likely, or at least possible, that there will be many variations of rite in the Mass of the future. But of this much we can be absolutely sure: the offering and the consecrating will remain the same. Wine will be put into the chalice, bread will be placed on the paten, and at the words of consecration the body and blood of Christ will be present. Nothing can alter this. From the first Mass, our Lord's, until the last Mass which shall be said before the end of the world, the material offering is made to stand before the Father and await the moment when the mystical slaying takes place. The material offering is not material only: it is moral as well. Now what is meant by this?

Put it this way. The real point about the bread and wine is not that it is good bread and expensive wine. In this particular kind of sacrifice the purely material value of the elements which are used, the wafer and the half cruet of perhaps cheap wine, hardly come into the story at all. It is not like the precious ointment which was spilled over our Lord's feet from the alabaster box, not like the costly libations of ancient rituals or the holocausts of animals for which considerable sums had to be paid: such 'sacrifices' suppose as an important feature the destruction or wasting of valuable material. A person offering such a sacrifice denies himself the possession of a certain good. He 'makes sacrifices' before he can do it at all.

But in the case of our sacrifice, the sacrifice of the Mass, the demand and the implication are quite different. The demand is not material but moral and spiritual: the demand for co-operation. The implication is that an entirely new value is set upon the act. Why is the offering of bread and wine so pleasing to God? Not because of what these things are but because of what they are going to be. The bread and wine will soon become the Body and Blood of Christ.

All the early part of the Mass is accordingly a looking forward. The priest, the faithful, the elements: they are waiting for a change to take place. The offertory is not a display of natural goods occupying a certain square space on an altar: it is a movement in the direction of a significant change—the change which we call transubstantiation. The replacing of one substance by another is the climax which fulfills the promise expressed in the offertory.

Transubstantiation is often called a 'conversion'. It is not such a theological term, and it is obviously far less specific. But from our point of view here, where it is not a question of theological study, the word 'conversion' serves a good purpose: it suggests the part we are to play in our co-operation. We are not subject to transubstantiation, but we are subjects of conversion. We can turn away from self and towards God. The Mass can transform us if we let it, can convert us so that we become more effective members of Christ's body. It can convert our material cares so that they become spiritual opportunities. It can convert the commonplace happenings of our day so that they become infinitely meritorious in the merits of Christ.

Theologians tell us that throughout our time on earth we are *in via*. Unless mortal sin interrupts our course and kills the life of the soul, we Christians are on our way to eternal life with God. All the time we are moving towards something. Life is a procession which does not stop until it reaches its destination in the eternal life of God. The Mass is a foretaste of all this: With the material elements offered on the paten and in the chalice, we human beings move toward our true destination, towards a climax from which there is no turning back.

7

# *The Place of Holy Communion*

We have seen on an earlier page that the appropriate time for receiving Holy Communion is during Mass. But since this involves something more important than suitable timing, the connection between the Christian sacrifice and the eucharistic sacrament deserves a short chapter of its own.

If the sacrifice is a common sacrifice, offered by all the faithful together and gaining graces which are shared by the whole mystical body, then eucharistic participation is a common action. It is a participation not only in the mystery of Christ's death but in the mystery of other people's lives. Though this is still the case when people receive our Lord outside the Mass, the idea of corporate life, corporate worship, corporate charity and growth is less in evidence.

The two mysteries, the one sacrificial and the other eucharistic, form a unity. Without restricting each one's efficacy—because the Mass is just as much the Mass if nobody except the priest receives Holy Communion, and Holy Communion is just as much Holy Communion when it is received privately and apart from Mass—the two mysteries complete one another.

Theologians, liturgists, scripture scholars and historians are always telling us how the sacrifice of the New Law took its cue from, and is the consummation of, the sacrifice of the Old Law. So we cannot do wrong in illustrating this theme which we are considering by taking a look at the most important sacrifice in the Hebrew year, the sacrifice of the Pasch.

The thing to notice here is that the Pasch was a feast as well as a sacrifice. Moreover a family feast. It had to be celebrated by the whole household gathered together at one time and in one place. There was no going off on one's own with one's own helping to keep the feast in one's own room. The sacrifice and the eating were linked together. The Paschal lamb (which had been slain earlier by the priests in the Temple) was the central figure, played the most important part, and those who stood around as witnesses were more than mere witnesses in that they shared and ate.

There is this too to be noted about the Paschal celebration: the participants were to think of themselves as being on a journey. They were dressed for travelling, carried staffs, and ate standing up—as we would eat at a counter on a railway platform. It was the feast of the Passover, a feast of movement. It was to remind them of how their ancestors had passed over the borders of Egypt, over the Red Sea, over the many obstacles which had separated them from their true home. It was not a feast of rest,

## The Place of Holy Communion

of sitting still, of arriving and having no further to go. The Mass, as we have seen, continues this idea: we are *in via*, on our way.

It is significant here that the Holy Communion which is given with the sacrament of the anointing of the sick is called 'viaticum' which is the Latin term for 'food on the journey'. The idea is that a journey which began with baptism is now, with death on the horizon, entering upon its last lap. So the traveller must be provided with something special to eat. His Holy Communion, it is true, is on this occasion received outside Mass. But death constitutes something of an exception. When the final obstacle is to be overcome an emergency usage comes into play. The form for the administration of Holy Viaticum differs slightly from that employed at Mass, the implication being that normally the recipient would be receiving our Lord at the altar and in its liturgical context but that this time ('just for today because you happen to be dying') he is at Mass in spirit: the altar is going out of its way to come to him.

Passing from the Old Testament to the New, a further illustration can be seen in an event which tradition regards as a foreshadowing of the Blessed Sacrament. By changing the water into wine at the marriage feast of Cana, our Lord was showing His power over material elements: He could alter their nature at will, transforming the substance of one into the substance of another. Notice the occasion of this miracle: an assembly when friends and relatives were gathered together in festive celebration. He could equally have worked the miracle in private, at home, to commemorate St. Joseph's birthday or as a surprise for Our Lady when she was having visitors.

Many reasons can be given for the choice of Cana and the wedding feast for this first demonstration of His supernatural authority over natural objects. A likely reason would seem to be that the guests at a wedding are drawn together in a rather special way: they come with a common intention of paying their respects to the bridal pair and of sharing this very important day with them. The guests become part of the family for the occasion—indeed part of the contracting families who are uniting in ties of a new kinship—and so are related to one another in their friendship for the married couple. They may not be aware that this bond exists, but if they work it out they will see that a wedding reception is different from a meal in a restaurant. Even if most of them are strangers to one another they are not like people who happen to be in the same hotel.

It is true that of the two the wedding is more important than the reception which follows it, just as it is true that the act of sacrifice is more important than the sacrificial communion which follows it, but what if the guests at Cana had wanted to record their appreciation privately and separately? Would our Lord have been pleased at Cana if a guest had told him "This is a rare and wonderful wine which you have given us instead of the water, so I will now pay you the compliment of taking it upstairs where I can concentrate better on the extraordinary thing that has happened, and where I can give undivided attention to this beautiful wine"?

Perhaps we feel sometimes that if we could take the Blessed Sacrament home with us, our Holy Communions would be less distracted and more pleasing to God. To think in this way is not wrong, because it is right to want to communicate with recollection, but by separating the notion of the sacrament from the notion of sacrifice it is all too easy to think of the sacrament as a private devotion.

To this it should be added at once, before a lynx-eyed student of early church history objects that at one time it was a perfectly normal thing for the faithful to carry the Blessed Sacrament back to their houses after Sunday Mass and give themselves Holy Communion on weekdays, that independent communicating was never considered to be a liturgical practice. It was a privilege prompted by two factors: persecution and the lack of weekday Mass. That the practice was looked upon as a departure from the eucharistic liturgical framework may be judged from the fact that for these domestic Holy Communions it was only under the form of bread that it was allowed at all. Holy Communion as administered during Mass at that time was always under both forms, bread and wine.

This may be the place to say a word about how Holy Communion was distributed in the early Church. At first it seems that the celebrant took the eucharistic bread which he had just broken at the altar, and gave it to the faithful who remained standing in their places. Then came the deacon or deacons carrying the chalice from which those who had received our Lord under one form were able to receive Him under the form of wine as well. In Eastern rites the same arrangement is still observed.

The Church is sometimes accused of denying the chalice to the laity at the time of the Reformation. Communion under one kind had come in long before that. From about 1100 it had become more and more rare in the West for lay people to drink from the chalice. In the case of Holy Communion for the sick, the chalice was never taken. The Church has always taught that our Lord is truly present in each element, and the reason why the point came to the fore particularly at the Reformation is that it became a test of true Catholicism. Schismatics demanded both forms: orthodox Catholics knew that in receiving the host alone they were receiving the whole Christ—body, blood, soul, divinity.

## 8

# 'It's Easier for You Priests'

The argument goes like this: the priest is trained to it, and can draw upon his theological knowledge when his interest begins to wear off. Even when actually saying Mass he has more to rivet his attention than the layman has. He is doing something all the time and has to keep his wits about him to get the rubrics right; the layman has nothing more to do than leave and resume his chair every now and then and is therefore at the mercy of stray distractions. The priest has a close-up view and touches the Blessed Sacrament: the layman sees little of what is going on, is often placed far away, and only if he is receiving Holy Communion does he come into close contact with the Blessed Sacrament.

Then there is the question of the liturgical languages, and familiarity with the psalms and those parts of scripture which are virtually unknown to lay people. The priest knows where to look for symbolism in the Mass, for echoes of an earlier tradition, for reminders and associations which are largely lost on a congregation. It is all very well, the layman complains not unreasonably, for the priest to talk about not letting the attention wander at Mass, about making the Mass live, about shaping one's daily life round the Mass, but the priesthood seems to have a way of making a man forget what it was like to be a layman.

Up to a point these objections will be valid for as long as there are priests to celebrate at the altar and lay people to attend from the body of the church. But if the liturgical spirit of the Second Vatican Council has its way, and at the moment of writing the signs are hopeful, such objections will become far less valid in the future than they have been in the past. With the Latin almost entirely confined to the prayers which the priest recites in a whisper, the language difficulty goes out. From being able to follow the parts which are said aloud, the layman will come to a deeper understanding of what has up to now been a confusion of biblical texts. This in turn will get him into the way of looking for associations and symbols of his own. And if more of the Mass is exposed to general view he will have nothing to complain about on the score of not knowing what is going on.

In every issue there is always room for further objection, so it is possible that someone may say at this point: 'Why not throw out Latin altogether? Why have any of the Mass prayers said in a whisper by the priest alone? Why keep the more obscure passages from the Old Testament when there are passages from the New Testament which are far easier to understand and which have a more direct bearing upon ordinary life? Why not do the thing thoroughly while you are about it, and give us a missal which we can read like a morning paper?'

Before these suggestions are examined it should be pointed out that the Mass is primarily something done rather than something said. For generations we have been talking about priests 'saying' Mass and 'singing' Mass; we have talked about the faithful 'hearing' Mass. This has tended to put more emphasis on the words spoken than on the act performed. It might have been better had we referred to priests 'offering' Mass, and the faithful 'attending' or 'assisting at' Mass. If too much importance is attached to the actual wording of the missal there is a danger that too little importance will be attached to the essentials of the Mass. The essential of the Mass is self-giving: first Christ's, then ours.

We can now take the zealous Catholic's proposals one by one. First, there is nothing especially holy about Latin. God does not listen more readily to Latin than to other languages. But on the other hand it has come to be the language of the Church, and the Church after all is the Bride of Christ. So why should not the Bride, when whispering to the Beloved, continue to use the language to which she has been accustomed? And if this should sound fanciful and far-fetched, remember that the idea derives from the inspired Canticle of Canticles.

While it is very much to be hoped that the new rite of offering the sacrifice of the Mass will be so simplified as to get rid of any suggestion of a mysterious code intelligible to none but the elect, it must also be conceded that the Church has every reason to hang on to its own language when she is, as it were, talking to herself.

## The Mass in Other Words

'Ah,' the zealous reformer will cry, 'but that's just what my second objection is about. If there were no secret prayers, then all the Masses could be in the vernacular. If the new rite is to be expressed intelligibly, then why can't the faithful take part in the whole of it? I thought the idea was that we should share more in what goes on.'

In order to answer this it is worth going back—which is what the modern liturgical movement is doing—and examining the question historically. What we call the Roman rite, expressed as it has been for centuries in Latin, emerged out of other rites and other languages. The Church began in Palestine and within the Roman Empire, so in the earliest expression of the Mass we trace two influences at work. The language in Palestine was Aramaic, the tradition was Hebrew. Our Lord spoke Aramaic, and so did the apostles. But with the coming of the Holy Spirit at Pentecost a new impulse was given to the Church which resulted in rapid expansion. Throughout the Roman Empire, predominantly Latin-speaking but Greek-speaking as well, the Christian religion established its centres and offered its Masses. While the essence of the Mass remained always the same, the language and ceremonial changed with the times and according to local custom. If you went into it scientifically you would find the Gauls, the Franks and even the Moors influencing the Western rite, while in the Eastern rite other tongues besides Syriac and Greek can be traced.

A number of prayers which we have today in the Latin rite began as private prayers which the celebrant could choose out of a book while something else in the ceremony was holding things up for him. These prayers were circulated throughout the Roman Empire, but eventually a definite list of them was prepared so that all priests were saying the same silent prayers when not reciting the public prayers out loud. In some Eastern rites the whole Canon is said out loud and this is because the altar is often screened off from the congregation who would not otherwise know what was going on.

All this has been introduced to show that even when the language of the Mass was a living language, the vernacular of the respective rite, there were prayers which the celebrant said privately and in which the congregation had no part. Most of the Mass as we know it now had become stabilised by the end of the seventh century. It had its silent or 'secret' prayers then, and there were still a few more to be added. It is worth remembering that the end of the seventh century, early as it sounds, represents over a third of the time which has elapsed between our Lord's day and our own.

Admittedly in the very early stages of the Church's life it was easier for the lay people to see the movements of the Mass, and therefore to take a more active part in the ceremony, but now that most Masses will be said while the priest faces the people, the visual difficulty will be reduced. Churches, moreover, are now being built with more regard for the faithful, enabling them to follow the priest's actions even from a distance. Mass shown in television is another help, making the layman familiar with the rubrics in a way which has never been possible before.

While it is the Church's intention to introduce the Mass to the layman and the layman to the Mass, it is not the Church's intention that the secular voice should dominate or dictate. Always it must be left to the Church to decide about points of worship as it must be left to the Church to decide about points of belief. In obedience and humility the layman takes what he gets. Sometimes the priest gets the impression that the layman is trying to take over and run the whole thing himself. The layman's function is a very real one, but subordinate. He plays a supporting role in the Mass's drama. He is more than an audience and less than the chief performer.

Let this be illustrated by an example drawn from the Mass itself. After the sacred elements of bread and wine, what is the most important thing on the altar? Most people would surely say the chalice. Not the altar cloth or candles, but the cup which for some of the time contains our Lord's Precious Blood. Few people would instinctively say the paten. Yet for some of the time during Mass the paten supports our Lord's body. We forget about the paten. This is partly because it is not much seen except by the celebrant and his ministers. At the elevation it is the chalice which is held up at the adoration of the Precious Blood: the paten is not elevated at the adoration of the host. The paten is covered during most of the Mass. It is either partly hidden under the corporal, or, if it is a high Mass, wholly hidden in the folds of the deacon's veil. For a minute or two it is covered by the purificator or mundatory. In the far-off days when Holy Communion was distributed under both kinds, the chalice and the paten, often a large plate of gold or silver, were in full view of the communicants. But when small hosts came to be used, the paten dwindled in size and was retired from public service.

## 'It's Easier for You Priests'

Today, unless Mass is said at a side altar and on occasions when there are few communicants, the paten is seldom used. What the lay people see as they receive Holy Communion is the ciborium which not only holds more hosts but goes back again into the tabernacle when the distribution is over. The part played by the paten then is important but secondary. A humble part. The celebrant makes the sign of the cross with it, kisses it, holds it in front of him at the offertory and upright on the altar after the *Pater Noster*, but I doubt that he thinks about it half as much as he thinks about the chalice. The layman can think of himself as a human paten: he has a function all right but it is not the most important of all.

Very well then, it may be easier for priests than for lay people. But just remember two things. First, the holiest actions, when repeated day after day, can cease to have the same impact: can cease to feel holy. The second thing to remember—and this is much more important—is that worship is not meant to be easy. However simplified by this or that liturgical reform, the Mass is still a mystery which calls for our faith, generosity, and patience. Essentially the Mass is sacrifice, inviting sacrifice in return.

9

# The Mass and Christian Unity

Up till now we have been considering the liturgy of the Mass in terms of how it affects us Catholics. Clearly the mind of the Church has first regard for her own members. Questions of language and ritual must be decided in the light of what is best for the spiritual life of the faithful. But there is also an apostolic side to the matter. The Mass is not just parochial: it is missionary and ecumenical.

Pope John's *aggiornamento* or "bringing into the modern context" has worldwide implications. The Pope's intention was more than merely to brush up, for home consumption, our inherited culture. The brushing up process, which was to range over fields of theological thinking and practical discipline, was designed to go beyond blowing the dust off our own produce so that we could sit back and eat at leisure without fear of competition from rival producers. Pope John, with his Second Vatican Council, was looking outwards every bit as much as he was looking inwards.

This is shown by the frequency with which words like 'encounter', 'exchange', 'dialogue' are used in the literature of the subject. Ecumenism means precisely that.

In such a scheme, envisaging a common understanding of worship as well as providing an open forum of discussion, the Mass holds an important place. Apart from its intercessory value—the infinite merits of Christ providing a deposit upon which mankind can endlessly draw—the Mass can show to members of other Christian bodies that we share a common understanding of what is meant by worship. With the essentials of the Mass made clear, and the language difficulty removed, we can much more easily bridge the gaps that separate us from other Christian denominations. Reformed sects will see in our Mass the primary element of homage which they see in their own. For their part they will not be so mystified as they have been, accusing us of mumbo-jombo and superstition, while for our part we shall not come to the folly of feeling superior about our unique privileges.

Look at it from the standpoint of the Protestant who is ready to keep an open mind about us. Whatever his particular church, he has probably inherited prejudices against Catholicism which are not easy to ignore. His study of history has built up a picture of a priest-ridden society, of a liturgy which appeals to the emotions, of an inflexible system which allows no liberty of expression, of a highly organised hierarchy in which the layman finds no place. This is the popular image, so it is hardly surprising that we have often met with bigotry among those who are pledged, as we are, to charity.

## The Mass and Christian Unity

So when the Protestant who is at all ready to co-operate and listen—no longer, since Pope John's time, a rarity—realises that our most representative act of worship is not a clerical monopoly after all but is a people's service, with laymen reading the lessons and deacons distributing Holy Communion, he will feel more at home with us. Our way of worship will not seem so very different from his own. Our approach to religion generally, and to worship in particular, will not only break down the barrier of strangeness, but will incline him to look out for further similarities, for further points of possible contact.

Until lately we Catholics have been both too sectarian in our attitude (which means too standoffish towards our separated Christian brethren) and too dependent upon ecclesiastical management. All the initiative has been left to the priests; no responsibility has been given to lay people. But a new mood is showing itself, and it is a healthy sign. Lay people are better instructed than they used to be, more interested in theological and liturgical things, less inhibited in their religious practice by social and economic distinctions. They are consequently well able to take upon themselves some of the duties, burdens and responsibilities which since the middle ages have been assumed by the clergy and almost identified with the clerical state.

If the ecumenical trend which has stirred such enthusiasm in its opening phases is to come to anything, the effort to reduce sectarian tension must come from laity, clergy, hierarchy alike. The tendency is for each one of these groups to leave all the work to the other two. Sectarian tension can be just as much an enemy to the ideal of the Christian family as racial or economic tension.

## The Mass in Other Words

In fact it is more of an enemy because it more directly affects divine charity. It does not matter so much when political parties sling mud at one another, and schools of art seem to exist for the purpose, but it matters a lot when Christian denominations squabble. The Mohammedans have a saying that, if you ask a Christian to explain his faith, you will get nothing but a tirade against other Christian faiths. We have come a long way from the day when Christians were recognised in a pagan world for the love which they bore one another.

It is because we Christians are a quarrelsome lot that we must make the most of the sacrament of love. The message which accompanied the birth of Christ, and which told of the peace to be found on earth by men of goodwill, referred as much to peace *among* the faithful as to peace *inside* them. If you go through the text of the Mass with a pencil and paper, noting down the references to peace, you will see how the Holy Eucharist, the central act of Christian worship, is as much concerned with peace as with mercy and petition. If the Mass commemorates the peace of the Nativity, it commemorates also the peace of the Resurrection. Peace is our Lord's greeting on Easter morning and at every reunion with His friends until the day of His Ascension, when He left it with them as something to be spread to all mankind.

This conception of peace, especially appropriate at a time when the unity of the Christian family is so much in people's minds, is well brought out in the rite of the kiss of peace which we have today at a sung Mass (and which perhaps may become part of every Mass). The custom goes back to the very beginnings of the Christian liturgy, deriving from the text in the fifth chapter of St. Matthew, where our Lord speaks of the need to sink our differences before coming up to offer our gifts at the altar. The offering will not be honored where there is enmity between brother and brother. It is the Sermon on the Mount that is in question here.

At first, as is still the case in the Eastern Church, the kiss of peace was given early in the ceremony. It was regarded as a preparation for the offertory, indeed for the whole eucharistic sacrifice, and as a pledge of good faith. Converts, on being received into the Church, were given the kiss of peace and so introduced to their first Holy Communion. It welcomed them into the unity of the Faith, heralding social as well as sacramental communion. The place of the kiss was accordingly transferred from its earlier position so as to link up more immediately with the reception of the Blessed Sacrament. The kiss of peace signifies the disposition, the actual communicating seals the union. No more divisions in the human family: peace settled among men of goodwill. Notice the theme as it is repeated in the *Libera* prayer after the *Pater Noster* (itself a prayer requiring the peace of mutual forgiveness if it is not to be invalidated), in the blessing *Pax Domini sit semper vobiscum* which follows, in the *Agnus Dei*, and in the prayers which the priest says bowing over the altar before the *Domine, non sum dignus*. From the moment of the blessing just mentioned (when the priest was making the three signs of the cross over the chalice with the particle of the Blessed Sacrament) until the eucharistic distribution, the faithful were turning in their places and giving one another the kiss of peace. The sign of unity which was made by the priest at the altar in a way which all could hear, even if they could not all see, was at the same time the signal for the congregation's profession of unity. It was a unity not confined to the congregation: it was a unity in which it was hoped that all would share.

10

# The Mass and the Rest of the Liturgy

From what we have seen, then, the Mass and the sacraments (particularly Holy Communion) reflect our social responsibility. As the Catholic becomes a mature Catholic in the modern world, he comes to see more of the liturgy's implication. In deepening his awareness, the liturgy deepens what is now often spoken of as his involvement or commitment. If it is true that "the day of private prayer behind a remote performing priest is bygone, or should be", as is the claim of Father John Halligan, C.M.F., then the day of a private morality behind a remote written code is bygone too, or should be. Our religion's engagement in the world of affairs finds its inspiration and source in an everyday liturgy, of which the Mass is the focal point.

Prayer and action go together. The liturgy and morals go together. If morals engage us every day, then we need the liturgy to engage us accordingly. It stands to reason that, if our prayer life is being conducted according to the spirit of God, our social life must follow the same course. The self which takes an active part in eucharistic worship cannot but be moved to take a correspondingly active part in communicating the life to others: the self loses its self-centeredness. The private self is private no longer: the home-grown is put up for general use. If we understand the liturgy properly, we cannot misunderstand social justice. The question of human rights is there, in the Mass.

The active participation of the faithful in a revised form of divine worship; an upgrading of biblical study; flexibility in ritual as a demonstration of respect for varying cultures. Such is roughly the meaning of the Liturgy Decree of the Second Vatican Council. It is what might be called a communitarian decree. It envisages two classes of men hitherto less considered by our religious leaders: the laity and the followers of other faiths. "A priest whose function is not extended by the co-operation of the laity" says Cardinal Suenens, "is a anomaly, a contradiction." And the great Jesuit theologian, Father Karl Rahner, a leading *peritus* or accredited adviser at the Council, writes in the same sense that "the clergy exists because there are laymen".

"The layman", Father Rahner says also, "is still generally understood in the Church as meaning the non-expert, the non-specialist in the Church. The word communicates nothing but the merely negative information that such a one is excluded from all office, dignity, and functions which belong to those who form the Church and represent it *vis-a-vis* the laity. Not because it is new or unheard of, but because the old truth has scarcely begun to penetrate our minds and hearts, we must declare and substantiate this single proposition: 'Through sacramental consecration and empowerment *every* Christian in the Church is constituted, qualified, and in duty bound to a position and task of active co-responsibility and work inside and outside the Church.'"

Two things emerge, then, very clearly from the conciliar deliberations and the resulting decrees. First, the Big Thaw in what had been for centuries a frosty front presented to non-Catholic bodies. Secondly the missionary commitment which rests with every baptised soul. The sense of community, rarely drawn attention to even as a quality to be looked for in a parish, is something which the Church of today is going all out to foster. Since the seeds of it are in baptism, it has its liturgical relevance. It is baptism, not ordination, which launches us on our mission. As members of Christ's body we are living in community. The tragedy is that we can get as far as this without living in unity as well.

Though this properly calls for a book on its own, a final word may be said upon the summons to a re-evaluation of scripture. "A warm and living love for the Bible must exist among the people of God if this restoration and adaptation are to revitalize the man of 1964 and after." The reading of the epistle and gospel in the vernacular at Mass, the exposition which is now compulsory on Sundays: this is as far as it goes at present. Proposals have been made, and seem to be gaining support, that there should be a serial course on New Testament readings at weekday Mass. A planned cycle for both New and Old Testament passages would certainly broaden the basis of the Mass, recalling its earlier function as giving instruction in addition to offering worship. The

Word laid open as well as the Word made flesh. Breaking the bread of the gospel before breaking the bread of the sacrament.

Though loyalty to the Church should guarantee our respect for the Liturgy Decree, we should know that it does not constitute an article of faith. It must be taken for what it is, and it does not set out to do more than regulate, exhort and make relevant a number of principles which over the centuries have lost their right perspective. It loosens old ground and sows new seed: it is not a magic formula: it will not produce a harvest either overnight or without industry on the part of those to whom it is addressed. Like many documents of its kind it is cautious, accommodating, ambivalent. It does not want to put people in bad faith. For this reason it steers between the extremely conservative and the extremely progressive views held by contemporary commentators. It may disappoint the diehard traditionalist and the firebrand reformer, but at least it opens doors and welcomes the daylight. Also, and this is surely something for those at each extreme to remember, it is only an interim decree. It promises new forms, for example, to be adopted in the administration of the sacraments of penance and confirmation. In the meantime, awaiting amplification, what is to be the reaction of the faithful?

Clearly what is *not* to be the reaction is the passive suspicion with which other legislative measures have at times been accepted. Still less may the reaction be one of active criticism. Just because it is a *ballon d'essai*, there is no excuse for trying to shoot it down. The Catholic who is looking for the will of God, who is doing his best to carry out the essential of the Mass in his own life, who sees the Church as the Bride of Christ, must surely want to extend the scope of his obedience. He will know that in doing so he is doing what the Decree itself is aiming to do. He is extending the influence of Christ's Church.

## 11

# *Summing Up*

Devout souls are sometimes heard to say, though with more piety than theology, that when they get to heaven they will miss hearing Mass and receiving Holy Communion. If they had listened to what was told them as children about heaven, Mass, and Holy Communion they would know that once they reach heaven they will not need the redemptive work of the Mass, and that eucharistic union will have given place to beatific union. They will need the merits of the Mass for as long as they are in purgatory, but, having attained the dimension of eternal life, they will not be in a position to miss anything.

The Mass has been a looking forward to the final consummation, the vision of God, and, since the end has now been achieved for them, the life of the blessed assumes the Passion, the Mass, the Holy Eucharist. To be in heaven and to have regrets of any sort is a contradiction in terms. If souls could feel at a loss in heaven without the Mass to hang onto as the central support of their religion, it would mean that their fulfillment had stopped short at our Lord's Passion and Death and had not gone on to the Resurrection. In this life the Mass is our strength and support; in the next life we shall not have to look for strength and support. The beatific vision will take care of all that.

What this book has tried to show is that the best way of learning the Mass, of learning to live by it, is to allow oneself to be used *with* it. The first thought should not be "what do I get out of it?" but "how do I come to think and act and pray according to it?" The soul who genuinely makes this second line of approach the primary consideration will learn soon enough how to proceed. Why? Simply because such an attitude supposes a mind and will which are wide open to the grace of the Holy Spirit.

We have tried to show moreover that religious problems, whether personal or affecting the Church as a whole, are best met by referring them to the Mass. The claim is not that the Mass answers every problem, but that it disposes towards *dealing* with every problem. The Mass is the *mysterium fidei*, the mystery of our faith, and faith means continuance in obedience, service, and conviction when sometimes the problems connected with it seem insoluble. If the Mass were called the "explanation of our faith" there would be an end to our search, but it is called the "mystery of our faith", so we go on trying to get closer when even the explanations fail us. Again, if the Mass were called the "mystery of our feelings" we might think that by forcing our emotions we could find what we are looking for on earth. But the

## Summing Up

Mass goes beyond feelings. Indeed, it tends to leave the feelings rather out of account. What the Mass asks for is co-operation, and this means cool deliberation. The human will surrendered with our Lord's to the will of the Father is worth any amount of emotional transport or mystical experience.

In the second half of the book we have gone on from the individual soul to the universal Church, and have suggested that the lessons of the Mass apply here too. By following out the implications of the daily liturgical sacrifice, the Church as well as its individual members can be seen to live the gospel to the fullest possible extent. The Church militant is all the time stretching out to "reach full stature in Jesus Christ". Its growth is seen in its never-ending activity of teaching, preaching, administering the sacraments, and above all of sacrificing.

At various stages in the Church's history it might have been thought that maturity had been reached at last, and that all the Church had to do now was to dig itself in and rest secure. But there has always been something more for the Church to do—sometimes in the world of philosophy and theology, sometimes in the world of social justice, sometimes in giving a lead when all other voices have been silent—and it looks as though today the Church is doing it fast. A living Church, an increasingly mature Church, a Church which has never stopped growing up and which will not be fully grown until Christ's second coming.

In the mercy and providence of God the future is never very clear at any time. Currently the future is about as uncertain as it has ever been. Nuclear power, the conflict of ideologies, the breakdown of trust among races, new interpretations of morality:

these things do not forecast an era of stability. But there are some things we can count on. We know that the gates of hell shall not prevail against Christ's Church, and that the Mass will go on being offered until the end of the world.

## About The Cenacle Press
## at Silverstream Priory

An apostolate of the Benedictine monastery of Silverstream Priory in Ireland, the mission of The Cenacle Press can be summed up in four words: *Quis ostendit nobis bona*—who will show us good things (Psalm 4:6)? In an age of confusion, ugliness, and sin, our aim is to show something of the Highest Good to every reader who picks up our books. More specifically, we believe that the treasury of the centuries-old Benedictine tradition and the beauty of holiness which has characterized so many of its followers through the ages has something beneficial, worthwhile, and encouraging in it for every believer.

cenaclepress.com

Also available from The Cenacle Press at Silverstream Priory

**Robert Hugh Benson**
*The King's Achievement*
*By What Authority*
*The Friendship of Christ*
*Papers of a Pariah*
*Confessions of a Convert*

**Blessed Columba Marmion OSB**
*Christ the Ideal of the Monk*
*Christ in His Mysteries*
*Words of Life On the*
*Margin of the Missal*

**Dom Pius De Hemptinne OSB**
*A Benedictine Soul: Biography,*
*Letters, and Spiritual Writings of*
*Dom Pius De Hemptinne*

**Dom Hubert Van Zeller OSB**
*Letters to A Soul*
*We Work While the Light Lasts*
*The Yoke of Divine Love*

**Dom Eugene Vandeur OSB**
*Hail Mary*

**Maurice Zundel**
*The Splendour of the Liturgy*

**Father Ryan T Sliwa**
*New Nazareth's In Us*

**Monks of Silverstream Priory**
*Dawn Tears, Spring Light, Rood*
*Peace: Poems*

cenaclepress.com

www.ingramcontent.com/pod-product-compliance
Lightning Source LLC
Chambersburg PA
CBHW060340080526
44584CB00013B/854